A Pillar Box Red Publication

In association with

THE BEST FOOTBALL MAGAZINE!

BARCELONA ANNUAL 2022

Written by
Jared Tinslay

Edited by
Stephen Fishlock

Designed by
Darryl Tooth

CONTENTS

SEASON REVIEW

We look back at BARCA's 2020-21 campaign month by month, checking out their biggest moments, star players and more!

SEPTEMBER

MEGA MOMENTS!

Messi transfer saga

Just a couple of weeks after handing in a transfer request that rocked the world of football, club captain and all-time legend Leo Messi announces that he'll stay for another season – although he says he was "forced" to stay! It ended a period of intense transfer speculation and fan protests!

Adios, Suarez

Messi might have stayed, but his best mate and partner up front, Luis Suarez, sealed a transfer to join La Liga rivals Atletico Madrid just before the start of the new campaign! It marked the end of a spell in which the striker scored 198 goals in 283 games for Barca – their third highest scorer ever!

Following two friendlies, La Liga finally kicked off at the end of the month, with Barcelona comfortably beating Villarreal in their opener at the Nou Camp! A four-minute brace from wonderkid Ansu Fati set Barca on their way, before Messi scored a penalty in Ronald Koeman's first competitive game in charge!

Fati celebrates

MAN OF THE MONTH!

ANSU FATI The 17-year-old academy gem was in inspirational form as he side-footed home the opener against Villarreal and then struck again with an ice-cool finish! He even won the penalty, which Messi stuck away, to cap off a perfect opener!

DID YOU KNOW?

Messi became only the sixth player to score a goal in 17 different La Liga seasons with his penalty on the opening weekend. Legend!

BARCELONA'S RESULTS

Date	Comp	Home	Score	Away
12/09	FRI	Barcelona	3-1	Gimnastic
16/09	FRI	Barcelona	3-1	Girona
27/09	LIGA	Barcelona	4-0	Villarreal

OCTOBER

MEGA MOMENTS!

Pedri opens his account

The trip to Turin to take on Juventus was billed as the Messi v Ronaldo battle – only for the Portugal megastar to miss out through injury! That didn't stop Leo from tucking away a penalty on his nemesis' home ground to seal the points!

Messi spot on

Barcelona's Champions League campaign kicked off with a commanding victory over Hungarian giants Ferencvaros! Messi scored in a joint-record 16th CL campaign, while 17-year-old midfielder Pedri netted his first senior goal for the club!

El Clasico clash

The season's first El Clasico didn't go to plan for Blaugrana supporters! A lively start to the game saw both teams score in the opening ten minutes, but second-half goals from Sergio Ramos and Luka Modric gave Real Madrid bragging rights at the Nou Camp!

MAN OF THE MONTH!

ANSU FATI The Spanish teenager became the youngest player to score in El Clasico this century and also the first player ever to score more than one Champions League goal before turning 18. The electric forward started the season on fire!

DID YOU KNOW?

Clement Lenglet and Gerard Pique received red cards in October versus Celta and Ferencvaros respectively!

BARCELONA'S RESULTS

01/10	LIGA	Celta Vigo	0-3	Barcelona
04/10	LIGA	Barcelona	1-1	Sevilla
17/10	LIGA	Getafe	1-0	Barcelona
20/10	CL	Barcelona	5-1	Ferencvaros
24/10	LIGA	Barcelona	1-3	Real Madrid
28/10	CL	Juventus	0-2	Barcelona
31/10	LIGA	Alaves	1-1	Barcelona

NOVEMBER

MEGA MOMENTS!

Super-sub Leo

It was a bad night in the capital when Barca visited Atletico's stadium! Not only did they lose and drop down to 10th in the league, but Gerard Pique picked up an injury that ruled him out for the rest of the calendar year and beyond!

Pique blow

Braithwaite double

Even without Messi in the squad, Barcelona managed to breeze past Dynamo Kiev at the end of the month to secure their spot in the knockout rounds of the Champions League, thanks to a brace from Denmark striker Martin Braithwaite!

After picking up just two points from their previous four league games, Barcelona needed to respond against Real Betis – and they did just that! Two goals and an assist from half-time substitute Messi turned the game on its head for a big win!

MAN OF THE MONTH!

ANTOINE GRIEZMANN Five goals and assists combined in five games for the France forward made him MATCH's pick for Barcelona's Player of the Month for November! One of his goals was a worldy volley against Osasuna as well, which won Barca's official Goal of the Month vote!

BARCELONA'S RESULTS

04/11	CL	Barcelona	2-1	Dynamo Kiev
07/11	LIGA	Barcelona	5-2	Real Betis
21/11	LIGA	Atletico Madrid	1-0	Barcelona
24/11	CL	Dynamo Kiev	0-4	Barcelona
29/11	LIGA	Barcelona	4-0	Osasuna

DID YOU KNOW?

In the 4-0 hammering of Dynamo Kiev, Ronald Koeman named Barca's youngest Champions League starting XI since December 2011!

DECEMBER

MEGA MOMENTS!

Cadiz upset

Forget the festive spirit, Barca fans must've felt like Scrooges after they saw their team beaten by newly promoted Cadiz at the start of the month! It was their first loss against them in La Liga since 1991!

BARCELONA'S RESULTS

Date	Comp	Home	Score	Away
02/12	CL	Ferencvaros	0-3	Barcelona
05/12	LIGA	Cadiz	2-1	Barcelona
08/12	CL	Barcelona	0-3	Juventus
13/12	LIGA	Barcelona	1-0	Levante
16/12	LIGA	Barcelona	2-1	Real Sociedad
19/12	LIGA	Barcelona	2-2	Valencia
22/12	LIGA	Real Valladolid	0-3	Barcelona
29/12	LIGA	Barcelona	1-1	Eibar

Things went from bad to worse for the Catalans when they lost top spot in their Champo League group to Juventus – with villain Ronaldo scoring two penalties at the Nou Camp in his first-ever group-stage encounter with Messi!

CR7 haunts Barca

Record breaker

The Argentinian magician still ended the month on a high, though – his goal against Real Valladolid broke Brazil legend Pele's record of the most goals for one club with his 644th net-buster for Los Cules. Wow!

MAN OF THE MONTH!

LIONEL MESSI There weren't any standout shows in December, but we're shouting out to La Pulga for writing his name in the history books by overtaking Pele! His winner against Levante was also class!

DID YOU KNOW?

Against Valladolid, Pedri became the third-youngest Barcelona player to record an assist in La Liga since the 1998-99 season, just behind Ansu Fati and Bojan!

JANUARY

MEGA MOMENTS!

Bilbao triumph in the Super Cup

After beating Real Sociedad in the semi-finals of the Spanish Super Cup, Barcelona twice let a lead slip against Athletic Bilbao in the final – with Messi getting sent off in the last minute of extra-time!

Lucky escape

Talking about extra-time, that's what it took for Barcelona to scrape past third-tier Cornella in the Copa del Rey – despite fielding the likes of Clement Lenglet, Miralem Pjanic and Antoine Griezmann!

Barcelona took on Athletic Bilbao for the third time in a month, and Leo Messi was once again in the headlines – but this time for all the right reasons! He scored a wonderful free-kick to bring up his 650th goal for the club!

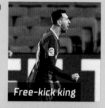
Free-kick king

MAN OF THE MONTH!

FRENKIE DE JONG Messi being suspended gave other players the chance to take the limelight – and De Jong was class all month! He hit the winner versus Huesca and also got a goal and assist against Elche!

DID YOU KNOW?

Messi's red card against Bilbao was the first of his Barca career on his 753rd appearance for the club!

BARCELONA'S RESULTS

Date	Comp	Home	Score	Away
03/01	LIGA	Huesca	0-1	Barcelona
06/01	LIGA	Athletic Bilbao	2-3	Barcelona
09/01	LIGA	Granada	0-4	Barcelona
13/01	SSC	Real Sociedad	1-1	Barcelona
18/01	SSC	Barcelona	2-3	Athletic Bilbao
21/01	CDR	Cornella	0-2	Barcelona
24/01	LIGA	Elche	0-2	Barcelona
27/01	CDR	Rayo Vallecano	1-2	Barcelona
31/01	LIGA	Barcelona	2-1	Athletic Bilbao

FEBRUARY

MEGA MOMENTS!

Barca's Copa del Rey match v Granada was way more exciting than it needed to be for Blaugrana fans! They were 2-0 down with just two minutes left to play, before Griezmann and Jordi Alba took the game to extra-time – where they scored another three goals!

Jordi Alba & Riqui Puig

BARCELONA'S RESULTS

03/02	CDR	Granada	3-5	Barcelona
07/02	LIGA	Real Betis	2-3	Barcelona
10/02	CDR	Sevilla	2-0	Barcelona
13/02	LIGA	Barcelona	5-1	Alaves
16/02	CL	Barcelona	1-4	PSG
21/02	LIGA	Barcelona	1-1	Cadiz
24/02	LIGA	Barcelona	3-0	Elche
27/02	LIGA	Sevilla	0-2	Barcelona

Barca's reward for coming back against Granada was a tough two-legged tie against Sevilla in the semi-final. Former hero Ivan Rakitic scored the second goal to put the Andalusians 2-0 up ahead of March's second leg...

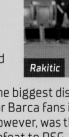
Rakitic

Mbappe

The biggest disappointment for Barca fans in February, however, was their 4-1 home defeat to PSG, with Kylian Mbappe tearing them to shreds with a sizzling hat-trick! It gave the French club a massive advantage going into the second leg!

MAN OF THE MONTH!

LIONEL MESSI Of course it was Leo! The superstar either scored or assisted in all but one of his eight games in February, ending the month with 11 goals or assists combined! His goal v Cadiz came on his club-record 506th La Liga appearance for Barca!

DID YOU KNOW?

Leo's goal v Sevilla at the end of the month was the eighth league game in a row that he'd busted net in – his best scoring streak in two years!

MARCH

MEGA MOMENTS!

Dramatic comeback

After losing the semi-final first leg v Sevilla 2-0, it was always going to take something special to recover at the Nou Camp – and that's exactly what Barca delivered! Gerard Pique scored in the 94th minute to take the game to extra-time, before Martin Braithwaite struck the winner. Drama!

BARCELONA'S RESULTS

03/03	CDR	Barcelona	3-0	Sevilla
06/03	LIGA	Osasuna	0-2	Barcelona
10/03	CL	PSG	1-1	Barcelona
15/03	LIGA	Barcelona	4-1	Huesca
21/03	LIGA	Real Sociedad	1-6	Barcelona

PSG tussle

It was too much to ask for Barcelona to produce two miraculous comebacks in the same month, though, with PSG holding on to a 1-1 draw in Parc des Princes to end the Spanish side's Champo League dreams for 2020-21. Ouch!

Koeman's team ended the month in style by thrashing Real Sociedad on their own patch! Leo Messi scored a brace as he celebrated a record-breaking 768th appearance for Barcelona, overtaking his old team-mate Xavi's all-time club record!

Leo the legend

MAN OF THE MONTH!

LIONEL MESSI In another mind-boggling month, Messi was directly involved in nine goals and assists combined in the five games across all comps! Shout out to right-back Sergino Dest too, who scored his first goals in a Blaugrana shirt against Sociedad!

DID YOU KNOW?

Teenage sensation Ilaix Moriba scored his first-ever goal for the club in the 2-0 victory over Osasuna!

APRIL

MEGA MOMENTS!

Mingueza nets in Clasico defeat

The rain poured down in Madrid on the night of the second El Clasico of the season, and the weather summed up Barcelona's mood by the end of the night! A second-half Oscar Mingueza goal simply wasn't enough to get them back in the match!

BARCELONA'S RESULTS

05/04	LIGA	Barcelona	1-0	Real Valladolid
10/04	LIGA	Real Madrid	2-1	Barcelona
17/04	CDR	Athletic Bilbao	0-4	Barcelona
22/04	LIGA	Barcelona	5-2	Getafe
25/04	LIGA	Villarreal	1-2	Barcelona
29/04	LIGA	Barcelona	1-2	Granada

Barca put their El Clasico misery well and truly behind them by sticking four goals past Athletic Bilbao in the final of the Copa del Rey! Messi scored a brace, including a stunning solo effort, as the Catalans breezed past Bilbao!

De Jong celebrates

High-fives

On the same day they announced they were hoping to join a new European Super League, Barcelona showed their superiority over Getafe to move up to third place in the league table – thanks to goals from Griezmann, Messi and Ronald Araujo!

MAN OF THE MONTH!

LIONEL MESSI It's worth looking up Messi's Copa del Rey final goals against Athletic Bilbao again on YouTube – even if you've watched them recently! He rolled back the years in that cup tie to prove that he can still perform at the highest level, and lifted the trophy proudly as captain of the club!

DID YOU KNOW?

April's Clasico defeat at the Bernabeu saw Real Madrid record three consecutive wins against Barcelona for the first time since 1978!

Copa del Rey winners

Trademark Messi free-kick

MAY

MEGA MOMENTS!

Barcelona came from behind to beat Valencia in a thriller at the Mestalla! Antoine Griezmann put Barca ahead before Messi clipped in a trademark free-kick to grab all three points for Los Cules!

Griezmann v Valencia

Barca's clash with Atletico was their chance to take control of the title race, but they couldn't break down a resolute Atleti defence, despite having seven shots on target. It also saw Luis Suarez face his old club for the first time since leaving!

Atletico hold firm

Lenglet sees red

Barcelona threw away a two-goal lead against Levante, then followed that up by losing their final home game of the season to Celta Vigo! Clement Lenglet was sent off for the second time in 2020-21 as Vigo scored a late winner!

MAN OF THE MONTH!

LIONEL MESSI It's that man again! Two goals against Valencia, plus strikes against Levante and Vigo, saw Messi reach 30+ league net-busters in a ninth different La Liga season, despite scoring just three goals in his first eight games of 2020-21!

DID YOU KNOW?

Barcelona lost more points from winning positions than any other team in La Liga since gameweek 32!

BARCELONA'S RESULTS

02/05	LIGA	Valencia	2-3	Barcelona
08/05	LIGA	Barcelona	0-0	Atletico Madrid
11/05	LIGA	Levante	3-3	Barcelona
16/05	LIGA	Barcelona	1-2	Celta Vigo
22/05	LIGA	Eibar	0-1	Barcelona

COPA KINGS!

The 2020-21 Copa del Rey victory was Barcelona's first piece of silverware since 2019! Check out the best stats and facts behind their success...

77%

Barcelona had 77% possession in the final against Athletic Bilbao and 14 shots on goal!

31

Barcelona got their hands on their 31st Copa del Rey trophy – an all-time record!

11

They've only missed two Copa del Rey finals in the last 11 campaigns. That's epic!

1

It was the first-ever time that Barca lifted the trophy in Seville's La Cartuja stadium!

56 Messi's brace made him the fourth all-time top scorer in Copa del Rey history!

35 It took Leo's trophy haul at Barcelona to 35 – more than any other player in the club's history!

1 It was the first trophy for Ronald Koeman as manager of Barca, although he also won the Copa once as a Barca player!

17 The Copa del Rey was a first trophy in Barcelona colours for 17 members of the squad!

5 It was also the fifth time in the last seven seasons that Barca have won the Copa!

FOOTY FLASHBACK

REAL MADRID 2
Higuain 14, Ramos 56

BARCELONA 6
Henry 18, 59 Puyol 20, Messi 36, 75, Pique 83

THE SCENE...

The 2008-09 season was in its business end! Barcelona were four points ahead of reigning champions and arch-rivals Real Madrid at the top of the table, but knew that defeat at the Bernabeu would leave them with just a one-point advantage going into the final four gameweeks. The Catalan club were hunting their first La Liga title since 2006...

MATCH FACTS!
DATE: MAY 2, 2009
GROUND: SANTIAGO BERNABEU, MADRID
ATTENDANCE: 79,500
MOTM: THIERRY HENRY

THE TEAMS...

Casillas

Ramos Cannavaro Metzelder Heinze

Robben Gago Diarra Marcelo

Higuain Raul

Henry Messi Eto'o

Iniesta Toure Xavi

Abidal Puyol Pique Dani Alves

Valdes

Gonzalo Higuain's opening goal was soon overturned as a Thierry Henry curler and a Carles Puyol header put Barca into the lead! It was from that moment that Barca ran Real ragged in front of their own fans, putting on an attacking masterclass to become the first away team in El Clasico history to score six goals and all but wrap up the title...

Puyol's celebration of holding his captain's armband aloft is one of the most iconic in Barca history!

WHAT CAME NEXT...

Barcelona travelled to London four days later to knock Chelsea out of the Champions League in dramatic fashion, thanks to a stoppage-time equaliser from Andres Iniesta, before winning the final 2-0 against Man. United in Rome! They also secured the La Liga trophy for the first time under Pep Guardiola and beat Athletic Bilbao in the Copa del Rey final!

WORDSEARCH

Can you find Barcelona's 2020-21 squad members in the grid?

```
I Z N N M O S D E P B I P B X J W A B S V A R Y Q U J N F A
W T H A O F E G H Q R N F N Y D P B M B L U A J P M B I N C
D Q I E R A O D I F A A G E Y B S Z D V N R Y Y E I H E M F
I B D A I T C E X G I Q T L Y A P P I G M G N O P R P W T N
K V H S B I V M T H T A Y R G N L R Z K N M Y L W M M U O U
N O D R A V H B N M H N K U J M O D B B U L Z F M Y Y S G L T
L S V D I H Z E F D W R S B V E L I A A R R C A B H W G P R
X D B S B N M L Z E A P Q O P P I T B Y M S D I Q G G S G I
R A R A U J O E M L I Y R O K N U J Y G S Y K A K Y G J G N
X J D U H P I R P A T U V N K Q G R B W U I F H U G T H T C
P I Q P V V T C X F E A V Q H K J U W F T C R L L Y K W E A
I U L A H I W M L U Z M V O K Q F H I I P W A U L H D J R O
W P F K H I E L A E A Y S T Z U S I T N O O H E U A Z T S U
T K Z J V P A I I N Q T E W X T T M R R G Z D U V B R C T D
Y O B Z U L I V D T K H E Z E L U E S P M E B C M A M O E A
U H W I P K D Q A E V K X U Z Q F F B O O V K N R Q P U G R
H M E N U D B I U N K Y Q N E T O M D E J O N G C B S T E N
O B E T E C U N D E U S C K B W E W I D J B M D A G G I N A
J P S S Y F G L K D U W T O F E A L L T T P M P L R Y N C U
O E L F S M E T I B V A W V C W F E O R U Q A I E I A H H F
D O Q G I I A N A H H G W J B H O S K J A D U V N E Z O O S
W T Q F E R N A N D E S N W Q B P B C D Q U Q X A Z O P Z B
L O J M J E G K Q V P J A N I C K R D E Y V Q N L M F O Z K
Y T T S X H Z T Y I Z K Q G S E F U Y J Y M Z R S A P N M P
R O V N A M A A Q H E I W S K A N B C O C S S Y Q N M U K V
R O B E R T O T U D S F N D C O L L A D O I Y M L N N N I U
Q F J Y A Z F U M R A M M I N G U E Z A N W D K D U T H W G
N K D B F L E N G L E T Q S K E U Q W C A N U F M M C Z X X
L A P N S A M D L G J Y W M P F N A P Y O I O Z L H J R K S
Q T U N E K B I H Z X H U M Q G B C N A Y U D V I Z W U K Z
```

Alba	Collado	Fati	Mingueza	Pjanic
Alena	Coutinho	Fernandes	Moriba	Puig
Araujo	De Jong	Firpo	Neto	Roberto
Arnau	De la Fuente	Griezmann	Pedri	Ter Stegen
Braithwaite	Dembele	Lenglet	Pena	Trincao
Busquets	Dest	Messi	Pique	Umtiti

ACTION REPLAY

How much can you remember about Barca's 2-0 CL away win over Juventus last season?

1 In which month did the two titans play – September or October?

2 Who played in goal for Barcelona – Marc-Andre ter Stegen or Neto?

3 True or False? Cristiano Ronaldo missed the match through injury!

4 What was the score at half-time?

5 Name the Barcelona winger who scored the opener in the 14th minute!

6 How did Lionel Messi score in stoppage time – a penalty or free-kick?

7 Who got sent off for Juve in the second half – Merih Demiral or Paulo Dybala?

8 True or False? The Serie A side failed to register a single shot on target!

9 Which team had over 55% possession of the ball – Juventus or Barcelona?

ANSWERS ON PAGE 60

MATCH compares Barca's amazing NOU CAMP stadium with Real Madrid's SANTIAGO BERNABEU to see which comes out on top...

CAPACITY

Barcelona's Nou Camp is the biggest club football stadium in the world, with a mind-boggling capacity of 99,354! That's over 17,000 more seats than the Bernabeu, so just imagine the difference in noise that those extra fans can make when they belt out the club's anthem before a game!

VERDICT: NOU CAMP WINS

NOU CAMP

RECORD ATTENDANCE

Back in 1986, in the quarter-finals of the European Cup, 120,000 supporters packed in to watch Barcelona take on Juventus at the Nou Camp! However, that record is over 9,000 fans short of the 129,690 spectators that witnessed Real Madrid take on AC Milan at the Bernabeu in 1956!

VERDICT: BERNABEU WINS

RENOVATIONS

Both stadiums are undergoing renovations, with Real Madrid turning their ground into a futuristic spaceship with a roof – although we're not sure why you'd need that in sunny Spain! The new Nou Camp will become a three-tiered super-stadium with a new capacity of over 105,000!

VERDICT: NOU CAMP WINS

TOURS

Both stadiums have really cool self-guided tours, where you can stroll around the stadiums and take in the changing rooms, player tunnels and interactive screens! However, at the Nou Camp there's also a part where you can put on headphones and teach yourself the club chant – as well as see the tiny chapel by the tunnel!

VERDICT: NOU CAMP WINS

BERNABEU!

ESTADIO SANTIAGO BERNABEU

HISTORY

The Bernabeu was built in 1947, ten years earlier than the Nou Camp! It was the first stadium in Europe to host both a European Championship and a World Cup Final and has seen four CL finals – compared with the Nou Camp's two! The Nou Camp was the venue for the 1992 Olympics football final, though!

VERDICT: BERNABEU WINS

VERDICT

Come on, you're reading a Barcelona Annual – you didn't actually think the Bernabeu would stand a chance, did you? Barca's stunning stadium is only gonna get more jaw-dropping once the renovations are completed, and we cannot wait!

VERDICT: NOU CAMP WINS

LIONEL MESSI'S...
BARCELONA

JOINS LA MASIA

December 2000

After a successful trial, the Barcelona bosses decided they wanted to sign a 13-year-old Messi from Argentina's Newell's Old Boys – and famously scribbled him a contract on a serviette! They also agreed to pay for the teenager's growth hormone treatment!

BARCELONA DEBUT

October 2004

Leo made his competitive debut versus none other than Barcelona's city rivals Espanyol, coming on as a sub in the 82nd minute. At the time, Messi became the club's youngest player in a competitive game at 17 years and 22 days old!

FIRST BARCA GOAL

May 2005

In the same season he earned his first senior start for Barca, Leo also made his Champions League debut and scored his first-ever goal for the club – the latter coming against Albacete and being assisted by Ronaldinho!

Scrapbook!

To celebrate Leo's record-breaking time at Barcelona, we take a trip down Messi memory lane to look back at his career highlights!

GOLDEN BOY AWARD

December 2005

The Golden Boy is a prize awarded to the planet's best young player aged 21 or under! Messi followed on from Rafael van der Vaart and Wayne Rooney to become the third star to win the prize in 2005!

EL CLASICO KING

March 2007

Scoring your first senior hat-trick is always going to be a special moment, but imagine doing it against your club's bitter rivals! Leo's first Barca treble earned a draw v Real Madrid, and he's since gone on to become El Clasico's all-time top scorer!

BEST GOAL EVER

April 2007

During the Copa del Rey semi-final against Getafe, Messi scored what would later be voted as the club's greatest-ever goal! He picked up the ball inside his own half, dribbled past five defenders before rounding the keeper and slotting the ball into the net!

CHAMPIONS LEAGUE WINNER

May 2009

Leo was part of the squad that won the 2006 Champo League, but played no part in the final, so 2009 was his first real taste of continental success with Barca! He headed into the clash with Man. United as the tournament's top scorer, and literally headed past Edwin van der Sar to help his club clinch the trophy!

DEBUT BALLON D'OR

December 2009

Leo didn't just win the 2009 Ballon d'Or vote... he smashed it! The 22-year-old earned 473 points – 240 more than second-placed Cristiano Ronaldo, which was a record margin of victory!

FIRST GOLDEN SHOE

September 2010

La Pulga ended the 2009-10 season with 34 league goals to help Barca clinch the title and finish as Europe's top goalscorer, winning the European Golden Shoe for the first time!

UNITED DEJA VU

May 2011

Man. United faced Barca again in the Champo League final in 2011, and again were beaten by a Messi goal! The Argentina ace was named Man of the Match for his performance and was the CL's top goalscorer again. Hero!

HISTORY MAKER

March 2012

March 2012 was a month to remember for Messi! Not only did he become the first-ever player to score five goals in a Champo League match – against Bayer Leverkusen – but he also became the club's all-time record goalscorer!

WORLD RECORD

December 2012

A mind-boggling year of goals saw the legend bust a total of 91 nets for Barca and Argentina in 2012! He was awarded a Guinness World Record for the most goals scored in a calendar year!

LA LIGA LEGEND

November 2014

Leo's scored more net-busters against Sevilla than any other opponent, but his hat-trick against them in November 2014 also saw him become La Liga's all-time top scorer – a record he's since added loads more goals to!

WICKED WORLDIES
May 2015

In May 2015, Messi scored one of the best goals of his career against Athletic Bilbao in the Copa del Rey final, picking the ball up near the halfway line and beating four defenders! He famously followed that up in June by sitting Bayern defender Jerome Boateng on the floor with a stunning piece of skill!

CAPTAIN FANTASTIC
May 2018

With the departure of legend Andres Iniesta, Messi was voted as Barcelona's new captain by his team-mates – and he only had to wait three months to lift his first trophy as skipper, after Barca beat Sevilla in the Spanish Super Cup!

SIXTH BALLON D'OR
December 2019

Cristiano Ronaldo and Lionel Messi have been mega rivals their entire careers, but Leo's followers had bragging rights after the star earned a record-breaking sixth Ballon d'Or in 2019 – one more than CR7!

TRANSFER REQUEST
August 2020

After a disappointing trophyless season, Messi decided he fancied a change of scenery in the summer of 2020 and handed in a transfer request! Fans of the club protested and begged him to stay, which he eventually did!

ANOTHER RECORD
December 2020

By scoring against Real Valladolid in December, Messi recorded his 644th goal for Barcelona, overtaking Brazilian legend Pele as the player with most goals for a single club!

MORE MILESTONES
March & April 2021

During the 6-1 demolition of Real Sociedad in March, Leo became Barca's all-time record appearance maker on 768 games! Then, a month later, he became the most decorated player for a single club by winning the Copa del Rey. Total legend!

GOODBYE, LEO
August 2021

In July, Messi agreed a new five-year deal to stay at the Nou Camp, but just a month later Barca announced that he'd be leaving the club due to 'financial obstacles'. During an emotional news conference, Messi said goodbye to Barca and the fans, "I don't want to leave this club – it's a club I love...I'm so sad."

MIND-BLOWING
You Tube CLIPS!

We check out some of the coolest videos on BARCELONA's official YouTube channel! Get a load of these class clips...

BARCELONA QR CODES EXPLAINED

This is a QR code – just scan it with your phone or tablet to watch each video clip on YouTube. Here's how to do it:

Download and install a free QR Code reader from the app or android store.

Hold your phone or tablet over the QR code and you'll be sent to the clip. Easy!

13

1:35 / 8:12

▶ #90secondschallenge

Rapid American right-back Sergino Dest is asked as many random questions as he can possibly answer in the space of 90 seconds, including who's got the best haircut in the squad, who his all-time Barcelona idol is, his favourite movie and whether he'd be up for doing a skydive. Get ready for LOLs!

▶ Magic Messi!

Lionel Messi scored a staggering 50th free-kick for Barcelona in their clash against Valencia last season, and this video looks back on some of his legendary set-piece stunners! Check out his laser-like accuracy!

1:35 / 8:12

▶ Next-Gen Nico!

Barcelona academy ace Nico Gonzalez is getting Cules supporters well excited after signing a new deal with a release clause of over £400 million! This awesome video shows off some of the midfielder's skills and tricks through the years! Top tekkers, mate!

▶ Whisper Challenge!

Netherlands midfield master Frenkie de Jong and Germany shot-stopper Marc-Andre ter Stegen take on Barca's famous Whisper Challenge, where one player has to mouth a phrase to another who's listening to music to see if they can make out what they're saying!

▶ Most Likely To...

Antoine Griezmann and Clement Lenglet give some insights into their team-mates' habits, like who's the most likely to share photos of their food on their squad group chat and who takes the longest to answer a message!

▶ Never Have I Ever...

...lost my phone, done the laundry or forgotten my passport! Those are some of the questions defenders Ronald Araujo and Oscar Mingueza had to answer when they took on Barcelona's Never Have I Ever game! Find out what they said by watching this mega funny clip!

▶ Champo League Champs!

Re-live Barcelona Femeni's epic Champions League final victory over English club Chelsea through these highlights – but look out for the related videos too, because there's some sick behind-the-scenes shots of some of their celebrations! "Campeones, campeones..."

SPOT THE DIFFERENCE

Study these Barcelona v Celta Vigo pictures really carefully, then see if you can find the ten differences between them!

NAME THE TEAM

Can you remember the stars that lined up in Barca's 1–1 draw with PSG in last season's Champions League last 16 clash?

1. Goalkeeper

2. Centre-back

3. Centre-back

4. Forward

5. Midfielder

6. Midfielder

7. Forward

8. Right-back

9. Midfielder

10. Forward

11. Left-back

ANSWERS ON PAGE 60

BARCELONA 3

Pedro 27, Messi 54, Villa 69

MAN. UNITED 1

Rooney 34

THE SCENE...

In a repeat of the 2009 Champions League final, Barcelona took on Man. United again just two years later, but this time at Wembley Stadium! Both teams entered the final as champions of their domestic leagues, so the game was billed as a rightful opportunity to crown the best team in Europe...

THE TEAMS...

Valdes

Dani Alves — Mascherano — Pique — Abidal

Iniesta — Busquets — Xavi

Villa — Messi — Pedro

Rooney — Hernandez

Park — Giggs — Carrick — Valencia

Evra — Ferdinand — Vidic — Fabio

Van der Sar

WHAT HAPPENED...

Man. United fell a goal behind thanks to a carving Xavi pass and a perfect Pedro finish, but equalised seven minutes later against the run of play through Wayne Rooney. The second half was pure dominance from Barca though, as they controlled over 60% possession, and were rewarded with two fine finishes from 20 yards out from forwards Leo Messi and David Villa to seal another CL victory over The Red Devils!

The result saw Barcelona win their fourth Champions League trophy – one more than opponents Man. United!

WHAT CAME NEXT...

WINNERS
UEFA SUPER CUP 2011

Legendary Man. United manager Sir Alex Ferguson said after the game that the Barca side of 2011 were the best team that his club have ever had to Face! Pep Guardiola's side went on to beat Porto in the UEFA Super Cup thanks to goals from Leo Messi and new signing from Arsenal Cesc Fabregas!

MATCH FACTS!

DATE: MAY 28, 2011
GROUND: WEMBLEY, LONDON
ATTENDANCE: 87,695
MOTM: LIONEL MESSI

BECOME A LEGEND!

Go all the way from La Masia to become a Barca legend! Use some coins as counters, grab a dice and battle your friends and family in this epic footy board game!

START ▶
KICK-OFF!
The player who rolls the highest number goes first!

2 ▶

3 ▶
LEGEND!
You've been scouted for Barcelona's La Masia academy! Move forward three spaces!

4 ▶

5 ▶
FAIL!
Your youth team coach says your diet needs to improve! Move back a space!

6 ▶

◀ 12
FAIL!
A terrible Twitter gaffe gets you some negative headlines! Move back a space!

◀ 11

◀ 10
FAIL!
You get nutmegged by Ansu Fati in training! Move back four spaces!

◀ 9

◀ 8
LEGEND!
You earn your first professional contract at Barca! Move forward three spaces!

◀ 7

13 ▶

14 ▶
LEGEND!
MATCH magazine profiles you as a "Wonderkid To Watch"! Move forward two spaces!

15 ▶
FAIL!
You miss out on your debut due to a niggling knee injury! Move back two spaces!

16 ▶

17 ▶

18 ▶
LEGEND!
You're brought on as a sub for Pedri for your debut in the Copa del Rey! Move forward four spaces!

◀ 24
LEGEND!
The fans invent a catchy new chant for you! Move forward two spaces!

◀ 23

◀ 22

◀ 21
LEGEND!
You score your first-ever goal for the club! Move forward two spaces!

◀ 20
FAIL!
All-time Barcelona legend David Villa criticises your potential! Move back one space!

◀ 19

25 ▶
FAIL!
You react badly to getting subbed and lose the fans' respect! Move back three spaces!

26 ▶

27 ▶
LEGEND!
You win the Young Player of the Year award! Move forward four spaces!

28 ▶

29 ▶
FAIL!
The manager tells you you're not training hard enough! Move back six spaces!

30 ▶
LEGEND!
You're given your favourite shirt number! Move forward one space!

◀ 36

◀ 35
LEGEND!
You score in the Champions League final! Move forward three spaces!

◀ 34
FAIL!
You get a record low score on a Barca quiz on their YouTube channel! Move back three spaces!

◀ 33

◀ 32
FAIL!
You conduct an interview in Spanish but get badly misquoted! Move back four spaces!

◀ 31

37 ▶
LEGEND!
You score a perfect hat-trick against Real Madrid! Move forward three spaces!

38 ▶

39 ▶
FAIL!
You try a Panenka penalty in El Clasico but the keeper saves it! Move back three spaces!

40 ▶

41 ▶
FAIL!
An old photo emerges of you as a child in full Real Madrid kit! Move back five spaces!

WINNER!
YOU'RE A BARCELONA LEGEND – YOU'LL GET A STATUE!

DESIGN A CLASICO SHIRT!

Last season, Barcelona released a special-edition shirt just for matches against arch-rivals Real Madrid, so we want you to design an El Clasico jersey for 2021-22 and the chance to win a jaw-dropping gaming bundle – an EPOS H3 Headset and a Nacon Pro Compact Controller! Get entering now...

TOP TIPS!

Make sure you avoid any Real Madrid colours, so no white on there!

Barcelona are sponsored by Nike, so don't forget the brand's Swoosh and the club crest!

We don't mind if you want to have an outrageous design or keep it simple!

Maybe include some of Barca's big wins v Real on the shirt somewhere!

EPOS

The lightweight, multi-platform EPOS H3 Headset delivers skin-tingling audio and extreme comfort for mega long gaming sessions!

For more info on this elite headset and other jaw-dropping gear, visit www.eposaudio.com

nacon

The Nacon Pro Compact Controller for Xbox boasts a range of customisable features like button mapping, adjustable sticks, trigger sensitivity and vibration motors!

For loads more info on this incredible controller and other cool gaming accessories, head over to nacongaming.com and follow @Nacon

HOW TO ENTER!

Send us a photo of your drawing via email or one of our social channels and we'll feature the best ones in MATCH magazine and on social media!

@ Email: match.magazine@kelsey.co.uk f facebook.com/matchmagazine
🐦 twitter.com/matchmagazine 📷 instagram.com/matchmagofficial

CLOSING DATE: JAN. 31, 2022

WHAT THEY

Barcelona's 2011 Champions League-winning side has gone down in history as one of the greatest teams in history! Here's what some of the stars went on to next...

JAVIER MASCHERANO

The ex-Liverpool and West Ham warrior stayed with Barcelona until 2018, tasting more CL success in 2015! He joined Chinese side Hebei China Fortune in 2018, before a short spell at Argentinian club Estudiantes. He now works as a representative for La Liga, helping to promote the Spanish league!

ERIC ABIDAL

The powerful left-back returned to Monaco in 2013 after more than a decade away since his first spell at the French club. A year later he joined Olympiakos, but retired from the game that same year. He returned to Barca as the club's director of football in 2018, but was sacked in 2020 following their huge defeat to Bayern Munich!

Barcelona won the league and Champions League double in 2010-11!

DANI ALVES

Dani Alves has won no fewer than 37 club trophies during his career, as well as two Copa Americas with Brazil! He ended his spell at Barcelona in 2016 to join Serie A side Juventus, but only lasted one title-winning season in Italy. He transferred to PSG in 2017, won two Ligue 1 trophies, before heading home to Sao Paulo to see out his career!

DID NEXT...

VICTOR VALDES

After notching up more than 380 league appearances in a Barca jersey, the flying shot-stopper fancied a move to Manchester! He joined United in 2015-16, but spent almost the entire season bench-warming. After a failed loan spell at Standard Liege and a random stint at Middlesbrough, he finally hung up his boots!

ANDRES INIESTA

Spain's World Cup winner in 2014 left his boyhood club Barcelona on the back of winning the 2018 Copa del Rey trophy as captain! He joined Japanese side Vissel Kobe and won the Emperor's Cup in his first season, before extending his contract in May 2021 to prolong his playing career until 2023!

DAVID VILLA

The lethal Spain striker had a fine three years at Barcelona, including scoring in that 2011 Champo League Final win! He left the club in 2013 to join rivals Atletico Madrid for a season, before a four-year spell at MLS side New York City. He finished his career at Japanese side Vissel Kobe, alongside old mate Iniesta!

XAVI

The midfield baller, who was known for his perfect passing, stayed at Barcelona until 2015. He joined Qatari club Al Sadd on a four-year deal where he won the league title in 2018-19. After hanging up his boots, he took over as manager and led the club to a domestic treble in his first season in charge!

PEDRI and ANSU FATI are the two most exciting youngsters in the Barcelona squad, so we've put them head-to-head to see which of the wicked wonderkids has the most potential...

PERFECT PEDRI!

When a player gets labelled the "next Andres Iniesta", you know they've got some talent – and when you watch Pedri taunt opposition defences with his dribbling and driving runs, the comparisons are clear. The Tenerife-born wonderkid admits that the legendary midfielder was his idol growing up – so much so that he once asked his dad if he could have the same haircut. The request was denied, but that didn't stop Pedri basing his game on the epic baller!

PEDRI

V

36

In 2020-21, Pedri became the youngest La Liga star with the most appearances in his debut top-flight campaign in the 21st century!

88

He finished the 2020-21 season with a mega impressive 88% pass completion rate!

2430+

No teenager played more minutes in La Liga last season than Pedri!

100

Against Osasuna last season, Pedri made 100 touches, becoming the youngest star to have over 100 touches in a single La Liga game since those records begun!

18

At 18 years old, he's the youngest player to score and assist a goal at Athletic Bilbao's San Mames stadium!

3

Pedri's the third-youngest player to assist a goal in La Liga in the 21st century!

FANTASTIC FATI!

Sevilla must be kicking themselves after Ansu Fati left their academy to join La Masia when he was just ten years old! They weren't able to convince him or his parents to stay with their youth set-up, but neither were Real Madrid, who were also keen on adding him to their academy a year earlier. Thankfully for Barca supporters, the mega exciting winger chose Catalonia over Madrid – and the rest, as they say, is history...

DID YOU KNOW?
When Fati and Pedri scored v Ferencvaros in October 2020, it was the first time in Champions League history that two 17-year-olds scored in the same game for the same team!

FATI!

16

In August 2019, Fati became the second-youngest player to debut for the club at just 16 years and 298 days old!

17

He's also Spain's youngest-ever scorer after busting net on his debut against Ukraine as a 17-year-old!

3

He's the youngest player to feature for Barca in the Champions League – and became the third-youngest star in its history on his debut!

21

His goal against rivals Real Madrid in 2020-21 made him the youngest El Clasico goalscorer in the 21st century!

1

His strike against Osasuna in August 2019 saw him become Barca's youngest-ever goalscorer and the third youngest scorer in La Liga history!

2

On his first start for Barca, he became the youngest player in La Liga's history to score and assist in the same match!

VERDICT!

Choosing between Pedri or Fati is like choosing between pizza or ice cream – they're different, but both total treats! Pedri's ever-presence in his first full season was totally unexpected, while Fati had to deal with loads of injuries in 2020-21. Rather than picking one or the other, we think they're gonna combine to help Barca transition into a new period of footy dominance!

TURN OVER FOR OUR LOWDOWN ON MORE BARCA WONDERKIDS!

RONALD ARAUJO

CENTRE-BACK

With Gerard Pique turning 35 in 2022, it's a good thing that Uruguay wonderkid Araujo has emerged! The powerful and rapid centre-back was actually hailed by Pique last season, who says he could be a Barcelona starter for the next ten to 15 years!

TOP SKILL: *Strength*

ROCKING REFRESH!

As well as Pedri and Ansu Fati, these Under-23 young guns are ready to help the club transition into a new period of football dominance!

INAKI PENA

GOALKEEPER

The young goalkeeper joined Barca's academy when he was 13 years old and famously saved six penalties against Atletico Madrid in an Under-14 tourno! He's developed into a really classy sweeper keeper for Barcelona's B side and could be the long-term replacement for Marc-Andre ter Stegen!

TOP SKILL: *Shot-stopping*

SERGINO DEST

RIGHT-BACK

Ever since Dani Alves left the club, Barca have been missing an attacking right-back who can really influence the game! Dest showed signs of potential in 2020-21, when he became the first American to play for the club. He's got competition this season though from the returning Emerson!

TOP SKILL: *Speed*

ARNAU COMAS
CENTRE-BACK

He was a solid ever-present for Barcelona B last season! The fair-haired CB could end up being the perfect long-term partner for Araujo or Mingueza at the heart of Barca's defence. He's a calm, composed and very intelligent defender with faultless positioning!

TOP SKILL:
Positioning

RIQUI PUIG
MIDFIELDER

Last season was a nightmare for Puig, with the classy midfielder making just two La Liga starts! Despite that, Barcelona still decided to renew his contract at the end of the season until 2023, highlighting that they still see potential in the midfielder compared with legend Xavi!

TOP SKILL: **Passing**

OSCAR MINGUEZA
CENTRE-BACK

MATCH reckons Mingueza is made to be the next Carles Puyol! Just like the Barca legend, Mingueza has progressed through the La Masia academy, impressed big time for Barca's B Team, can play as a right-back or a centre-back, and even has the long locks!

TOP SKILL:
Awareness

INSIDE LA MASIA!

Take a look inside La Masia – Barcelona's world-famous youth academy – where young players live and train!

The outside of the building has Barca's motto – Mes Que Un Club – on the side!

The video room is used to analyse games or training – or maybe to watch films!

Players share bedrooms but each have their own TV, desk and an area to study!

There's a Barcelona v Real Madrid-themed table football, as well as an electric race kart and pool table!

The Play and TV Zone has big screens, comfy sofas and a table tennis table!

FOOTY FLASHBACK

JUVENTUS 1
Morata 55

BARCELONA 3
Rakitic 4, Suarez 68, Neymar 90+7

THE SCENE...

These two teams came into the 2015 Champions League final with the chance of winning a continental treble – both had just won their leagues and domestic cups! Barca, under Luis Enrique, were spearheaded by the jaw-dropping MSN front-line of Lionel Messi, Luis Suarez and Neymar, while Juventus had one of the world's fiercest defences...

THE TEAMS...

Buffon

Lichtsteiner · Bonucci · Barzagli · Evra

Pirlo

Marchisio · Vidal · Pogba

Morata · Tevez

Neymar · Suarez · Messi

Iniesta · Busquets · Rakitic

Alba · Pique · Mascherano · Dani Alves

Ter Stegen

MATCH FACTS!
DATE: JUNE 6, 2015
GROUND: OLYMPIASTADION, BERLIN
ATTENDANCE: 70,442
MOTM: ANDRES INIESTA

WHAT HAPPENED...

It didn't take long for Barca to break Juve's defensive wall, but the opener within the first four minutes came from midfielder Ivan Rakitic rather than the MSN trident! Juve equalised ten minutes into the second half after Alvaro Morata pounced on a rebound, but Barca rallied, re-took the lead through Suarez and then killed the game off on the counter in stoppage time!

Rakitic's opener was Barcelona's fastest-ever goal in a Champions League Final!

WHAT CAME NEXT...

Barcelona celebrated becoming the first team in history to secure two continental trebles, but said goodbye to legendary midfielder Xavi who'd played his last game for the club. Luis Enrique's side followed up their CL success by beating La Liga rivals Sevilla 5-4 after extra-time in a thrilling UEFA Super Cup clash!

EL CLASICO HISTORY

We take a closer look at the Barca v Real rivalry over the years!

DI STEFANO SHOCK!

Argentina ace Alfredo Di Stefano was on the verge of signing for Barcelona back in 1953, with the club even flying him and his family to Europe. However, Real Madrid smelled blood and argued they'd also agreed to sign him. FIFA said they'd have to share the player over the course of four seasons, which Barca rejected – only for him to become an all-time Real legend!

FIRST CLASICO!

The year 1902 was one to remember for Barcelona fans! Not only did they win their first-ever trophy – the Copa Macaya, contested between Catalan clubs – but they also won the first Clasico in history! The game was played in Madrid, and Real went ahead, but Barca came back to win 3-1!

1943

1953

1983

1902

COPA DEL GENERALISIMO!

In 1943, Barca met Real Madrid in the semi-finals of the Copa del Generalisimo – known today as the Copa del Rey! After winning the first leg 3-0, Barca fell to a jaw-dropping 11-1 second-leg loss. Reports later suggested that the Barca players were threatened and warned not to win the match – or else!

MARADONA MAGIC!

Real fans obviously knew how to appreciate Argentinian talent after Di Stefano's spell at the club, but nobody expected to see them applauding Barcelona's Diego Maradona score a goal – especially at the Santiago Bernabeu! But that's what happened after the magician rounded the Real keeper before scoring in 1983!

MESSI v CR7!

When Cristiano Ronaldo completed his world-record transfer from Man. United to Real Madrid in 2009, he also kick-started one of the most epic individual battles in football history! Over the next decade, he tussled with Leo Messi for La Liga's top scorer awards, Ballons d'Or and GOAT debates!

ICONIC CELEBRATION!

There have been some action-packed games and iconic goals throughout the years, but one of the most memorable moments in recent history came during their clash in April 2017! Messi scored a 92nd-minute winner in a topsy-turvy game, and celebrated by taking off his shirt and holding it aloft in front of the Real fans at the Bernabeu!

FIGO FURORE!

Portugal winger Luis Figo was a fans' favourite at the Nou Camp – that is, until he decided to leave to join arch-rivals Real Madrid! The capital club paid a world-record fee for his services, but that didn't soften the blow for Barca fans, who showed their hatred by throwing a pig's head at the player when he returned to their stadium as a Real star!

2011

2017

2000

2009

2021

GLOBAL GAME!

Nowadays, El Clasico is one of the most highly-anticipated matches in the football calendar, with their 2021 April clash viewed in a total of 182 countries with a potential audience of around 650 million! It's the hottest rivalry on the planet!

2005

ROCKING RONALDINHO!

Real Madrid fans applauding a Barca star scoring a goal was expected to be a once-in-a-lifetime occurrence, but Brazilian baller Ronaldinho got Los Blancos supporters on their feet once more after his sensational showing at the Bernabeu in 2005 – including scoring a jaw-dropping solo stunner!

FAMILIAR FOES!

It all got a bit heated in 2011 when Jose Mourinho's Real Madrid and Pep Guardiola's Barcelona faced each other four times in the space of 18 days – in the Copa del Rey Final, the league and the Champions League semi-final! They drew in La Liga, Real won the cup clash, but Barca got through to the CL Final – where they beat Man. United!

BARCA'S NEW BOYS!

Get to know three of Barcelona's awesome free summer signings – *MEMPHIS DEPAY, ERIC GARCIA* and *SERGIO AGUERO* – a little bit better!

GARCIA

BEN TORNAT
ERIC GARCIA

DID YOU KNOW? Garcia won the European Championship at U17 and U19 level for Spain!

beko

ONE OF THEIR OWN!

Just like club legend Gerard Pique, Eric Garcia was very nearly one that got away! He joined La Masia when he was seven, but left ten years later to join Man. City. During his first season in England he captained their Under-18s team and then made his full debut in December 2018. Thankfully for Barca, he decided he wanted to return to Spain and rejected City's contract extension!

DUTCH DNA!

Memphis Depay joins a long list of Dutch players to feature for Barcelona, including the likes of current team-mate Frenkie de Jong, all-time legend Johan Cruyff, famous twins Ronald and Frank de Boer, and his current manager Ronald Koeman! In fact, Depay becomes the 21st player from the Netherlands to represent the club – let's hope he creates his own legacy during his spell in Catalonia!

DEPAY

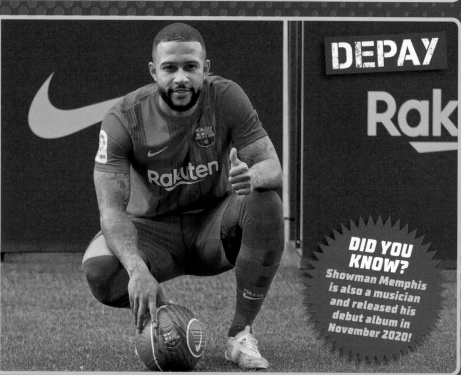

Rak

DID YOU KNOW? Showman Memphis is also a musician and released his debut album in November 2020!

AGUERO

MESSI REPLACEMENT?

When Sergio Aguero signed for Barcelona, he was hoping to play alongside best buddy Lionel Messi, but now he'll have to try to replace him! The Premier League's highest-scoring foreign player of all time is an absolute goal machine, but even he will find it difficult to replicate the number of goals Messi racked up season upon season at the Nou Camp!

best free transfers!

Depay, Garcia and Aguero all signed for nothing, so MATCH takes a look at some of Barca's best-ever free transfers!

Luis Enrique
From Real Madrid ★ 1996

Barca supporters weren't sure when Luis Enrique signed from their huge rivals, but he won over their hearts by scoring versus Los Blancos and becoming club captain!

Phillip Cocu
From PSV ★ 1998

Cocu spent six successful years at the Nou Camp, became club captain and left as Barca's record holder for the most league appearances by a foreign player!

Giovanni van Bronckhorst
From Arsenal ★ 2004

Gio was converted from a midfielder to a left-back and soon became a huge fans' favourite at Barca, starring in their 2006 Champions League final win versus The Gunners!

Henrik Larsson
From Celtic ★ 2004

The Sweden legend won two league titles and the Champions League in two seasons at the club, and was involved in both goals in the 2006 CL final win over Arsenal!

Mark van Bommel
From PSV ★ 2005

Van Bommel was a holding midfielder who spent one very successful season at the club, starting in the 2006 Champo League final win, before being sold to Bayern for £6m!

STAT ATTACK!

Get a load of **BARCELONA**'s record league appearance makers, Ballon d'Or winners, social media followers and tons more!

192

Lionel Messi registered a La Liga–high 192 assists for Barcelona – including nine in 2020-21. Legend!

62

No team kept more possession in 2020-21 than Barcelona's 62% – and they were also the league's most accurate passers!

HOW THEY SCORED IN LA LIGA IN 2020-21

HEAD
7

LEFT FOOT
54

RIGHT FOOT
19

TOP BARCA LA LIGA APPEARANCE MAKERS

Player	Appearances
Lionel Messi	520
Xavi	505
Andres Iniesta	442
Sergio Busquets	415
Carles Puyol	392

94%

Gerard Pique had an incredible 94% pass completion rate in the 2020-21 season – higher than any other team-mate!

CHAMPIONS LEAGUE RECORD
ALL-TIME

PLAYED
265

WON
156

GOALS
586

94
CM

DE JONG

92 PAC   95 DRI
85 SHO   90 DEF
92 PAS   91 PHY

1.1M+

That's how many coins you'll need to buy Frenkie de Jong's POTS FIFA card!

5

Sergio Busquets assisted Lionel Messi five times in 2020–21 – no other duo combined for more goals in La Liga last season!

6 Number of Barcelona Ballon d'Or winners!

Luis Suarez
1960

Rivaldo
1999

Johan Cruyff
1973 & 1974

Ronaldinho
2005

Hristo Stoichkov
1994

Lionel Messi
2009, 2010, 2011, 2012, 2015 & 2019

FCB

Barcelona's club crest was chosen over 100 years ago after they held a competition in 1910 among its members to design a new crest!

PEDRI V FATI

Breakthrough Seasons For Barca

GAMES	44
GOALS	4
ASSISTS	5

GAMES	39
GOALS	13
ASSISTS	3

Rakuten

FC Barcelona
@fcbarcelona · Sports team

facebook
103m+
LIKES

fcbarcelona

97m+
FOLLOWERS

Stats only include official matches. Correct up to end of 2020-21 La Liga season.

BARCELONA BRAIN-BUSTER!

How well do you know the Catalan club?

1. Which La Liga rivals did Barcelona sign Antoine Griezmann from in 2019?

2. True or False? Pep Guardiola used to be a rock-solid centre-back for Barcelona!

3. Which French club did Barca Femeni beat in the semi-finals of the 2020-21 Champo League?

4. What was the main colour of the club's third kit in 2020-21 – pink or yellow?

5. What was the aggregate score of both La Liga Clasicos in 2020-21?

6. What year did Jordi Alba join Barca – 2008, 2012 or 2014?

7. Which country does Femeni baller Lieke Martens play for?

8. Who was manager of Barcelona before Dutch gaffer Ronald Koeman?

9. True or False? The Nou Camp is the largest football stadium in Europe!

10. Which of these isn't one of Barca's nicknames – Blaugrana, Los Cules or Los Blancos?

1 ....
2 ....
3 ....
4 ....
5 ....
6 ....
7 ....
8 ....
9 ....
10 ....

WORDFIT

Fit 25 of the club's top appearance makers into the huge grid!

Alba	Bakero	Iniesta	Ramallets	Sergi
Alexanko	Busquets	Messi	Rexach	Torres
Alves	Cesar	Migueli	Rife	Valdes
Amor	Gallego	Pique	Sadurni	Xavi
Asensi	Guardiola	Puyol	Segarra	Zubizarreta

ANSWERS ON PAGE 60

BARCELONA 6

Suarez 3, Kurzawa 40 [og], Messi 50 [pen], Neymar 88, 90+1 [pen], Roberto 90+5

PSG 1

Cavani 62

THE SCENE...

It was the 2016-17 Champions League round of 16. PSG had just thrashed Barcelona 4-0 at home in the first leg of their knockout round tie, thanks to a brace from Angel di Maria and goals from Edinson Cavani and Julian Draxler! The Parisians were expected to stroll through to the quarter-finals, but the Nou Camp giants had other ideas...

THE TEAMS...

Ter Stegen

Umtiti   Pique   Mascherano

Iniesta   Busquets   Rakitic

Neymar   Messi   Rafinha

Suarez

Cavani

Draxler   Verratti   Lucas

Rabiot   Matuidi

Kurzawa   T.Silva   Marquinhos   Meunier

Trapp

MATCH FACTS!

DATE: MARCH 8, 2017
GROUND: NOU CAMP, BARCELONA
ATTENDANCE: 96,290
MOTM: NEYMAR

"La Remontada" translates to "The Comeback" in Spanish – and is used in the country to refer to Barca's 2017 comeback v PSG!

WHAT HAPPENED...

Barca went 3-0 ahead after 50 minutes, but were struck a killer blow in the 62nd minute when Cavani scored a crucial away goal – or so they thought! The home side rallied for a final push and managed to score three times in the last seven minutes to turn the game on its head – including an iconic, last-gasp strike from Sergi Roberto in the 95th minute!

WHAT CAME NEXT...

It ended up being all for nothing for Barca! The Catalan club were hammered 3-0 in the quarter-finals by Juventus in the first leg, and were unable to stage a similar Nou Camp comeback twice in one year. Their win over PSG will always be one of the greatest Champions League nights in history and one of those "Where were you?" moments in football!

FANTASTIC

Barcelona Femeni **completed the continental treble last season,** winning the *Primera Division, Copa de la Reina* **and** *Champions League!* **Here are the best stats and facts behind their record-breaking season...**

1 Barca became the first-ever club to get their hands on both the Men's and Women's Champions League trophy!

6 Striker Jenni Hermoso finished as the joint-top scorer in the 2020–21 CL with six net-busters!

4 Barcelona's 4-0 win against Chelsea was the biggest margin of victory in any single-legged Women's Champo League final!

29 They completed the league season with 87 points – winning 29 out of 30 games, losing just once!

6 They got their hands on their sixth league title, overtaking Athletic Club in the all-time charts!

FEMENI!

145

They busted 145 Primera Division nets in 2020-21 – no other team hit more than 74 league goals!

9

Barcelona beat Santa Teresa and Deportivo 9-0 at home in the league last season!

8

Barca Femeni's Copa de la Reina victory v Levante was the eighth time they lifted the trophy – more than any other club in history!

TURN OVER FOR OUR EPIC LIEKE MARTENS PROFILE!

MARTENS

DUTCH DYNAMITE

The lethal Netherlands forward has transformed Barcelona.

July 12, 2017 is when everything changed for Barcelona Femeni. The club had only existed professionally for two years, but they were ready to announce their first-ever paid for signing – Rosengard and Netherlands international Lieke Martens. During her presentation to the Barcelona supporters, she announced that her aim at the club was to win many titles and, of course, have great success in the Champions League too. Four years and nine trophies later, climaxing in last season's incredible final victory over Chelsea, it's safe to say that she has been true to her word. A star on and off the pitch, the classy Netherlands forward has already created a lasting legacy at the Catalan club...

BARCELONA DREAMS

Martens grew up in the south of the Netherlands and started to play football when she was five years old. As a child, she always dreamed of playing for Barcelona and was a big fan of Brazilian trickster Ronaldinho. She'd watch clips of him embarrassing defenders and then head to the garden to try to replicate his skills. As proof that hard work pays off, she now gets to wear the same colours and kit that her idol and legendary trickster used to wear as a player!

AWESOME AWARDS

A few weeks after signing for Barcelona, Martens made her mark on the international scene. She scored three goals at the 2017 UEFA Women's European Championship for the Netherlands to win the Bronze Boot, including a net-buster in the final against Denmark, and was later named in the Team of the Tournament and the competition's Best Player. Later that year, she was named the UEFA Women's Player of the Year for her jaw-dropping Euros performances!

CHAMPION CULE

When Barca landed Lieke, they were hoping she'd help deliver a first league title since 2015 and swing the balance back in the club's favour. They finished one point behind Atletico Madrid in 2017-18 and six points behind in 2018-19, but finally got their hands on the title in 2019-20 and easily retained the crown in 2020-21. Since she's been at the club, they've also won two Copas de la Reina, one Supercopa Femenina – and obviously the Champions League!

THE MARTENS FINAL

When you look back at most great finals, there's normally one protagonist who takes centre stage and steals the show and, against Chelsea in the 2021 Champions League final, that person was Martens! She tore The Blues' defence to pieces on numerous occasions and was involved in the build up to all four of Barcelona's goals, putting the ball on a plate perfectly for Caroline Graham Hansen for the fourth. It was one of the best individual displays in Barca Femeni history!

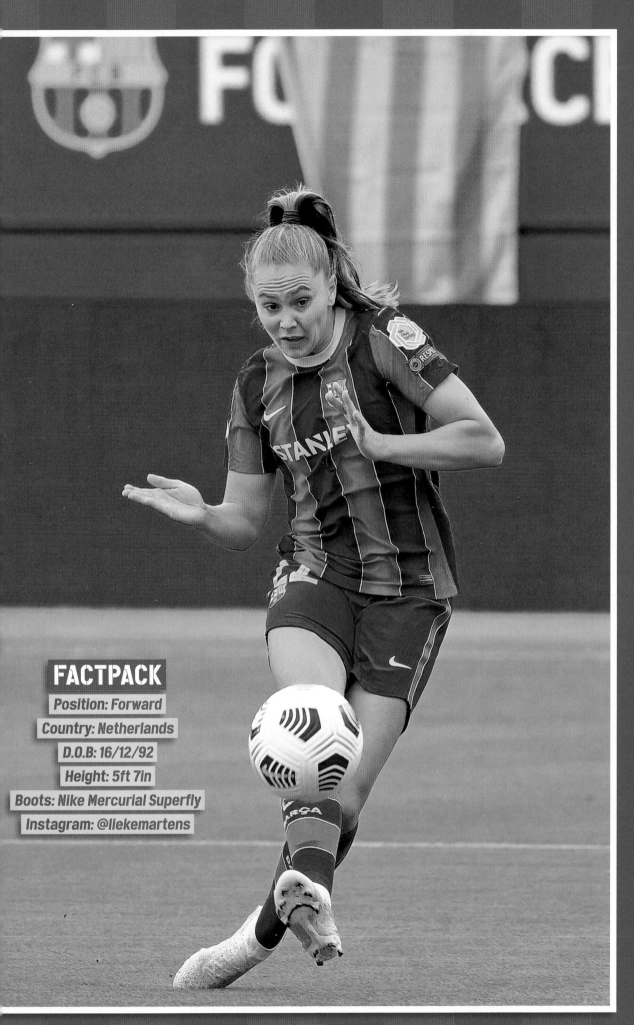

FACTPACK

Position: Forward
Country: Netherlands
D.O.B: 16/12/92
Height: 5ft 7in
Boots: Nike Mercurial Superfly
Instagram: @liekemartens

2021-22 HOME SHIRT

MATCH takes a closer looks at Barca's 2021-22 home threads...

"The fans have taken me as their own since I joined and it's amazing to see a jersey which captures the identity and values of such a wonderful club!"
Frenkie de Jong, Barca midfielder

The club shorts are half blue and half garnet, and pair with matching striped socks!

FAVE KITS!

In 2019, Barca asked fans to vote for their favourite home kits! Check out the top three...

1ST

2014-15

The Messi, Suarez and Neymar trident tore it up in these threads and won the club's second continental treble!

2ND

2008-09

This shirt was inspired by Barca's first-ever kit, which was half-and-half! They also won the treble this season!

3RD

2016-17

Barca failed to win the league or Champions League this season, but fans still respected Nike's effort!

MEET THE MANAGER

RONALD KOEMAN

Get the complete lowdown on the gaffer in charge of BARCELONA...

FIRST TROPHY!

Koeman lost his first-ever cup final in charge of Los Cules in the Spanish Super Cup in January 2021 against Athletic Bilbao, but got his revenge a few months later. Barca thrashed Bilbao 4-0 in May in the Copa del Rey final to see him lift his first trophy as gaffer in Spain!

PAST PLAYER!

The Dutchman joined Barcelona from PSV in 1989 and became a real fans' favourite during his spell in Catalonia! The versatile defender, who could also play in midfield, won four league titles as a player and scored the winner in the 1992 European Cup final!

"He has a lot of knowledge about football because I think he understands the game and was a great player before!"
Frenkie de Jong
Barcelona midfielder

FORCA KOEMAN!

Fans in the Netherlands got a real treat at the start of 2021 after a TV channel released a new documentary – Forca Koeman – about the first six months of his reign at Barcelona. It followed his journey from Dutch national team coach to the Nou Camp!

MAGIC MARKSMAN!

Even though he was mostly a defender, Koeman was lethal in front of goal! In fact, he's still the top-scoring defender in world footy, with 90 goals for Barca in all competitions. He was known as the 'King of Free-Kicks' for his incredible dead-ball ability!

STAT ATTACK!

Take a look at some of Koeman's stats from his first season in charge!

34
He won 34 of his first 54 games in charge of Barca with a win rate of 62.9% – however, he lost his first Clasico 3-1 against Real Madrid!

1
His win rate at Barca in his first season was the highest of his entire career as a gaffer, which includes spells at PSV, Ajax and Netherlands!

122
Barca hit 122 goals in Koeman's first full season in charge – including 85 in La Liga alone – an average of over two goals per game!

52
No player featured more times for Barca under Ronald Koeman in 2020-21 than Pedri's 52 games – and all that in his first season at the club!

Wordsearch — P18

Action Replay — P19

1. October
2. Neto
3. True
4. Juventus 0-1 Barcelona
5. Ousmane Dembele
6. A penalty
7. Merih Demiral
8. True
9. Barcelona

Spot The Difference — P30

Name The Team — P31

1. Marc-Andre ter Stegen
2. Clement Lenglet
3. Oscar Mingueza
4. Ousmane Dembele
5. Sergio Busquets
6. Frenkie de Jong
7. Lionel Messi
8. Sergino Dest
9. Pedri
10. Antoine Griezmann
11. Jordi Alba

Brain-Buster — P50

1. Atletico Madrid
2. False – he was a midfielder
3. PSG
4. Pink
5. Barcelona 2-5 Real Madrid
6. 2012
7. Netherlands
8. Quique Setien
9. True
10. Los Blancos

Wordfit — P51

LOVE MATCH?
GET IT DELIVERED EVERY FORTNIGHT!

THE UK'S ONLY WEEKLY FOOTBALL MAGAZINE!

2 PACKS 12 CARDS IN TOTAL!

Premier League 2020/21 ADRENALYN XL OFFICIAL TRADING CARDS!

MATCH!

» GIFTS! » GIFTS! »

CHAMPIONS LEAGUE... GOAL MACHINES!

6 ISSUES FOR JUST £6!*

PACKED EVERY ISSUE WITH...

★ Red-hot gear

★ News & gossip

★ Stats & quizzes

★ Massive stars

★ Posters & pics

& loads more!

HOW TO SUBSCRIBE TO MATCH!

CALL 📱
01959 543 747
QUOTE: MATBA22

ONLINE 🖱
SHOP.KELSEY.CO.UK/ MATBA22

ROLL OF HONOUR

CHAMPIONS LEAGUE
1991-92, 2005-06, 2008-09, 2010-11, 2014-15

FIFA CLUB WORLD CUP
2009, 2011, 2015

EUROPEAN CUP WINNERS' CUP
1978-79, 1981-82, 1988-89, 1996-97

FAIRS CUP
1957-58, 1959-60, 1965-66 (won outright in 1971)

EUROPEAN SUPER CUP
1992, 1997, 2009, 2011, 2015

LA LIGA
1928-29, 1944-45, 1947-48, 1948-49, 1951-52, 1952-53,
1958-59, 1959-60, 1973-74, 1984-85, 1990-91, 1991-92,
1992-93, 1993-94, 1997-98, 1998-99, 2004-05, 2005-06,
2008-09, 2009-10, 2010-11, 2012-13, 2014-15, 2015-16,
2017-18, 2018-19

COPA DEL REY
1909-10, 1911-12, 1912-13, 1919-20, 1921-22, 1924-25, 1925-26,
1927-28, 1941-42, 1950-51, 1951-52, 1952-53, 1956-57,1958-59,
1962-63, 1967-68, 1970-71, 1977-78, 1980-81, 1982-83,
1987-88, 1989-90, 1996-97, 1997-98, 2008-09, 2011-12,
2014-15, 2015-16, 2016-17, 2017-18, 2020-21

SPANISH SUPER CUP
1983, 1991, 1992, 1994, 1996, 2005, 2006, 2009,
2010, 2011, 2013, 2016, 2018

SPANISH LEAGUE CUP
1982-83, 1985-86

SMALL WORLD CUP
1957

LATIN CUP
1949, 1952

PYRENEES CUP
1910, 1911, 1912, 1913

MEDITERRANEAN LEAGUE
1937

CATALAN LEAGUE
1937-38

CATALAN LEAGUE CHAMPIONSHIP
1901-02, 1902-03, 1904-05, 1908-09, 1909-10, 1910-11,
1912-13, 1915-16, 1918-19, 1919-20, 1920-21, 1921-22, 1923-24,
1924-25, 1925-26, 1926-27, 1927-28, 1929-30, 1930-31,
1931-32, 1934-35, 1935-36, 1937-38 (includes Copa
Macaya 1901-02 and Copa Barcelona 1902-03)

CATALAN SUPER CUP
2014-15

CATALAN CUP
1990-91, 1992-93, 1999-2000, 2003-04, 2004-05, 2006-07,
2012-13, 2013-14 (until 1993-94, Copa Generalitat)

EVA DUARTE CUP
1948-49, 1951-52, 1952-53